Pet Questions and Answers

PET FISH

Questions and Answers

by Christina Mia Gardeski

raintree

a Capstone company — publishers for children

Raintree is an imprint of Capstone Global Library Limited, a company incorporated in England and Wales
having its registered office at 264 Banbury Road, Oxford, OX2 7DY – Registered company number: 6695582

www.raintree.co.uk
myorders@raintree.co.uk

Text © Capstone Global Library Limited 2017
The moral rights of the proprietor have been asserted.

Edited by Carrie Braulick Sheely and Michelle Hasselius
Designed by Kayla Rossow
Picture research by Pam Mitsakos
Production by Gene Bentdahl

ISBN 978 1 4747 2140 0
20 19 18 17 16
10 9 8 7 6 5 4 3 2 1

British Library Cataloguing in Publication Data
A full catalogue record for this book is available from the British Library.

Every effort has been made to contact copyright holders of material reproduced in this book. Any omissions
will be rectified in subsequent printings if notice is given to the publisher.

All the internet addresses (URLs) given in this book were valid at the time of going to press. However, due
to the dynamic nature of the internet, some addresses may have changed, or sites may have changed or
ceased to exist since publication. While the author and publisher regret any inconvenience this may cause
readers, no responsibility for any such changes can be accepted by either the author or the publisher.

Acknowledgements

Alamy Images: roger askew, 21; Shutterstock: AndreJakubik, 5, carnival, 9, Moo teaforthree, 17, Nikiparonak,
1, 22, Nipon Laicharoenchokchai, 11, oksankash, 19, Pavel Vakhrushev, cover, Photoman29, 13, S-F, 15,
voylodyon, 7

Contents

Who can breathe under water?

My fish! Fish breathe through gills. Water carries gas called oxygen to the gills. The oxygen goes into the blood and through the fish's body. Fish need oxygen to live.

gill

How do fish swim?

Fish wave their bodies back and forth to swim. Their tail fin pushes them through the water. Other fins help them to turn or stop.

tail fin

Can fish smell?

Fish smell through two small holes on their heads. Water flows fast through these holes. The smells in the water tell a fish if food or danger is near by.

Do fish have ears?

Fish do not have ears on their heads.

They have ear parts inside their bodies.

Fish have lines on their sides called cells.

These cells help the fish to know when

something moves near by.

What do fish eat?

Pet fish eat fish flakes or frozen food made from plants and animals. Do not feed your fish too much! This will make the fish ill. It also makes the water dirty.

Where can I keep my fish?

Pet fish live in fish tanks filled with water. A pump keeps the water moving. A filter keeps the water clean.

Do fish sleep?

Fish do not sleep like humans or other animals. They rest and save energy. Some fish settle down at the bottom of a tank. Other fish float in one spot.

Can I train my fish?

Most fish are clever.
They can be trained to do
simple tricks. Some fish will
swim through hoops for treats.

Can I handle my fish?

Do not handle your fish. You may hurt it. Your hands can make the water dirty. Enjoy your fish from outside its home.

Glossary

energy strength to do active things without getting tired

filter machine that cleans liquids or gases as they pass through it; a filter cleans the water in a fish tank

fin body part that fish use to swim and steer in water

flake small, thin piece of something

gill body part on the side of a fish; fish use their gills to breathe

handle pick up with your hands

oxygen colourless gas; humans and animals need oxygen to breathe

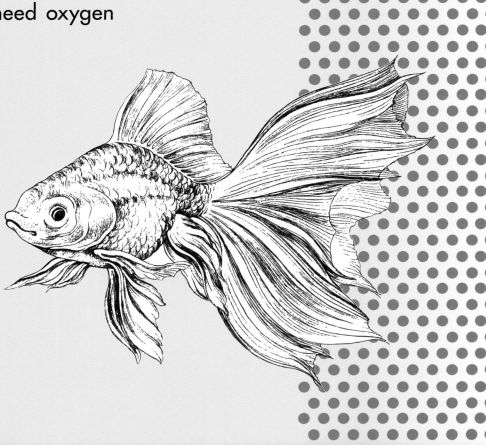

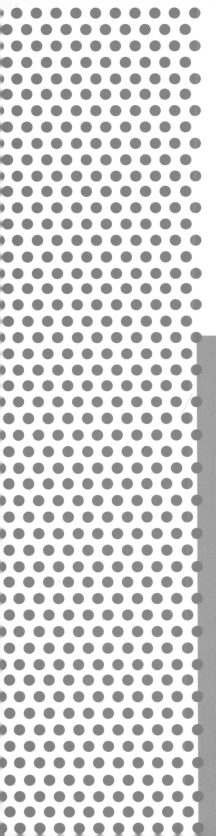

Read more

Fish (Animal Classification), Angela Royston (Raintree, 2015)

Fish Body Parts (Animal Body Parts), Clare Lewis
(Raintree, 2015)

Goldie's Guide to Caring for your Fish (Pets' Guides),
Anita Ganeri (Raintree, 2015)

Websites

www.bbc.co.uk/nature/animals/by/fish
Discover more about all types of fish.

www.dkfindout.com/uk/animals-and-nature/pet-care
Find out more about pet care.

Comprehension questions

1. Explain how fish breathe.

2. Fish tanks have filters. What are filters?

3. How do fish rest?

Index